THE UNKNOWN KURT WEILL

(1900-1950)

A Collection of 14 Songs

Edited by Lys Symonette

as sung by
TERESA STRATAS

(Nonesuch Record D-79019)

..OPEAN AMERICAN MUSIC CORPORATION

CONTENTS

Among all of the songs (dating from 1925 to 1944) in this volume, Lotte Lenya's favorite was *Nanna's Lied*. Although it had been written for her, she never attempted to sing it. She had an incredible modesty about her own work and would joke about the way Weill used to say to her "How did you get away with that?"

Knowing Weill's innermost concerns and intents better than anyone else, she realized that deep down he loved the classically trained operatic voice. She was always disturbed when Weill's songs were referred to as "Cabaret Songs" and often stated that Weill never wrote a single song for the cabaret. She always referred to them as "Art Songs" and felt that in their pure and simple wealth of melody they resembled Schubert songs more than any others.

Teresa Statas' masterful recording (Nonesuch D-79019) of the songs contained in this volume seemed to her proof of this point. Tragically, Lenya did not live long enough to see this publication. As her close friend of thirty years, I can truthfully say that she would consider it an invaluable contribution to and an enrichment of the currently available music in print by one of the true giants of 20th-Century music.

New York, June 1982   Lys Symonette

THE GERMAN SONGS
English synopses by Kim H. Kowalke

NANNA'S LIED
(Nanna's Song)

1
Gentlemen, I was only seventeen when I landed on the love market. And I learned a lot of things—mostly bad, but that was the game. Still I resented much of it. (After all, I am a human being.)
Thank God, it all goes by quickly—both the love and sorrow. Where are the tears of last night? Where are the snows of years gone by?
2
As the years go by, it gets easier on the love market—easier to embrace a whole troop there. But it's amazing how your feelings cool off when you're stingy with them. (After all, everything gets used up eventually.)
Thank God it all goes by quickly—both the love and sorrow. Where are the tears of last night? Where are the snows of years gone by?
3
And although you learn the tricks of the trade on the love market, it's never easy to convert lust into small change. Still it can be done, but meanwhile you get a little older. (After all, you can't stay seventeen forever.)
Thank God it all goes by quickly—both the love and sorrow. Where are the tears of last night? Where are the snows of years gone by?

KLOPS-LIED
(Meatball Song)

Here I'm sitting eating meatballs. A sudden knock. I look around, surprised. I'm wondering. . .All of a sudden the door is open. I'm thinking "How come? " The door was shut, but now it's open. I go out and take a look. Who's standing there? It's me, it's me, it's me!

BERLIN IM LICHT-SONG
(Berlin in Lights-Song)

Sunshine may be enough when you go for a walk, but the sun isn't enough to light up the city of Berlin. It's no little hick-town, it's one helluva city! If you want to see everything there, you've got to use a few watts. So what then? What kind of a city is it?
Come on, turn on the lights so we can see what there is to see. Come on, turn on the lights and don't say another word. Come on, turn on the lights so we can see for sure what the big deal is: Berlin in Lights.

UND WAS BEKAM DES SOLDATEN WEIB?
(What Did the Soldier's Wife Receive?)

And what did the soldier's wife receive from the ancient capital Prague? From Prague she received high-heeled shoes—a greeting and high-heeled shoes.

And what did the soldier's wife receive from Oslo across the sound? From Oslo she received a little fur piece and the hope that it would please.

And what did the soldier's wife recieve from wealthy Amsterdam? From Amsterdam she received a hat—she looks good in that Dutch hat.

And what did the soldier's wife receive from Brussels, Belgium? From Brussels she received the rarest of lace—oh, to own Belgian lace.

And what did the soldier's wife receive from Bucharest in the south? From Bucharest she received a strange, gay, Rumanian smock.

And what did the soldier's wife receive from vast Russia? From Russia she received the widow's veil for the funeral.

DIE MUSCHEL VON MARGATE
(The Mussel of Margate)

On the Promenade in Margate there was a picture of a big mussel on a tin sign in front of a souvenir stand. There an old man peddled painted mussels. All of Margate knew his pitch: Shell! Shell! Shell!

The mussel of Margate will bring you luck, the mussel made out of gold. If you catch a glimpse of it, you'll remember many an unforgettable hour.

On the Promenade in Margate there was really quite a stench. An oil rig has replaced the mussel shop. The son of that old man started up another business, a syndicate for naphtha and gasoline: Shell! Shell! Shell!

The mussel of Margate brought him good luck, the mussel made out of gold. Whenever he saw it, he happily remembered many unforgettable gushers.

And when they began to pump on the Promenade in Margate, a dozen hung on every drilling rig over oil in Baku, Koltschak, and Denikin. Blood turns into gasoline there. From a thousand throats burst forth the cry: Shell! Shell! Shell!

The mussel of Margate brings them good luck, the mussel made out of gold. Whenever they see it, they recall many a speech in the League of Nations.

And when the sun rose to its highest point on the Promenade in Margate, the oil started to burn. From Aserbeischan to Tibet it set the world on fire. Oil is the name of our Fatherland. For its sake, we'll drill our hides to bits: Shell! Shell! Shell!

The mussel of Margate brings them good luck, but we're going to the dogs! When we look at the mussel of Margate, remember that in that last decisive hour we'll all pay the price.

WIE LANGE NOCH?
(How Much Longer?)

I will confess there was a night when I willingly gave myself to you. You took me and drove me out of my
mind. I believed that I could not live without you.

You promised me blue skies, and I cared for you like my
own father. You tormented me, you tore me apart.
I would have put the world at your feet.

Look at me, will you! When will I ever be able to tell
you: It's over. When that day comes. . .I dread it. How
much longer? How much longer? How long?

I believed you. I was in a daze from all of your talk and
your promises. I did whatever you wanted. Wherever
you wanted to go, I was willing to follow.

You promised me blue skies, and I—I didn't even dare to
cry. But you have broken your word and your vows. I
have been silent and tortured myself.

Look at me, will you! When will I ever be able to tell
you: It's over. When that day comes. . .I dread it. How
much longer? How much longer? How long?

DER ABSCHIEDSBRIEF
(The Farewell Letter)

For two full hours now I've been sitting in the Cafe
Bauer. If you're no longer interested, then tell me to
my face! My cream won't turn sour just because of
that. To hell with you, my sweetheart. So what?
Let's call it quits. You mustn't think that I'll miss you.
We're all washed up. Even I have what they call "honor."
Don't show up again, my darling, or I'll throw you out.

You're not the first one to disappear like that. I don't
deserve that kind of treatment, sonny. Do you actually
think that I couldn't replace you? There are plenty of
better fish in the sea.

I'm wearing the green poplin dress—the one that has a
hole in it, thanks to you. You know how revealing it is.
Also, I still have a pillowcase that I started for you.
You were supposed to get it on Christmas Eve. That's
all over now, and all the same to me. Others will sleep
on it—more than once. Because what's over, sweetheart, is gone for good.

I'm not proud. The situation doesn't call for that. If
you've got some money, send it fast. A bald-headed
man is sitting across from me and leering. That's the
boss from Engelhorn's Hotel! Well, what do you know!
The gentleman across the table just asked if I would like
to...—because he would very much like to... He has
cash, the old crook. Keep your money! And sleep by
yourself, my boy!

You're just like them all. The old fogey is coming over.
He's going to take me with him...So, bug off! Kiss my
ass! With all my heart, your friend, Erna Schmidt.

ES REGNET
(It's Raining)

I ask nothing, I must not ask. You have told me not to.
But do I hear your car? Then I think, should I say
something? Or should I say nothing? It's all said in
your look. Do you believe that only the mouth speaks?
Eyes are like windows. One can always see through any
window. And if you close them, everything seems
worse. My eyes hear something different from my ears.
I was born to bear pain. Let me look through the window. Let me look! The sun can no longer shine. "It's
raining," says the window. It says only what it thinks.
Let us weep together!

DAS LIED VON DEN BRAUNEN INSELN
(Song of the Brown Islands)

This is the song of the Brown Islands. The men are evil
and women sick. A lady-ape does business there, and
the fields are withering in the stench of oil.

Are you going there, Freddy? Not me, Teddy. The dollar alone won't make me happy. Are you going there,
Freddy? Not me, Teddy. If I want to see apes, I'll go
to the zoo.

These are the Brown Islands, my boy! The women are
sick, and the men are evil. A lady-ape keeps the whole
thing going. The ones who come here are healthy, but
those who leave have lost their guts.

Are you going there Freddy? Not me, Teddy. The dollar alone won't make me happy. Are you going there,
Freddy? Not me, Teddy. If I want to see apes, I'll go
to the zoo.

Those who go there are healthy, but those who leave
have lost their guts. The lady-ape rules in bed and in the
factory too. She has money, and she's always right. The
menfolk do as they're told, both in bed and in the
factory.

Are you going there, Freddy? Not me, Teddy. The dollar alone won't make me happy. Are you going there,
Freddy? Not me Teddy. If I want to see apes, I'll go
to the zoo.

Petroleum stinks and the island stinks. It stinks of yel-
low and black men. But the dollar doesn't stink, because oil brings cash and nobody can compete with the
lady-ape.

Are you going there, Freddy? Not me, Teddy. The dollar alone won't make me happy. Are you going there,
Freddy? Not me, Teddy. If I want to see apes, I'll go
to the zoo.

THE FRENCH SONGS
English synopses by Susan Grayson

YOUKALI: TANGO HABANERA

Wandering at the will of the sea, my vagabond bark led me to the end of the world. It's quite a small island, but the sprite who dwells there politely invites us to tour it.

Youkali is the land of our desires. It means happiness and pleasure; it is the land where we leave cares behind. It is the beacon in our clouded night, the star we follow; it's Youkali. There we keep our promises. It is the land of shared love. It means the hope in all human hearts, the rescue we all wait for. Youkali is the land of our desires. It means happiness and pleasure, but it's only a dream, a folly. There is no Youkali.

And life, tedious and banal, drags us along. Yet the poor human soul, seeking oblivion everywhere, knew how, in leaving this earth, to find the mystery where our dreams are buried, in some Youkali.

Youkali is the land of our desires. It means happiness and pleasure; it is the land where we leave cares behind. It is the beacon in our clouded night, the star we follow; it's Youkali. There we keep our promises. It is the land of shared love. It means the hope in all human hearts, the rescue we all wait for. Youkali is the land of our desires. It mean happiness and pleasure, but it's only a dream, a folly. There is no Youkali.

JE NE T'AIME PAS
(I Don't Love You)

Take away your hand. I don't love you, for it's what you wanted—you're just a friend. Your embracing arms, your dear kiss, your sleeping head are all for others. When it's evening, don't speak to me intimately with that low voice. And above all, don't give me your handkerchief. It holds too much of the perfume I adore. Tell me of your loves—I don't love you—of your most seductive hour—I don't love you. And if the other one loved you or was ungrateful, don't be charming when you tell me; I don't love you.

I didn't cry, I didn't suffer, for it was just a dream, a folly. It's enough for me that your eyes are clear without regret of that evening or melancholy; it's enough to see your happiness, your smile. Tell me how your heart was captured, tell me even the unspeakable. No be quiet. I'm on my knees, the fire has died, the door's closed. I don't love you. Don't ask anything, I'm crying, that's all. I don't love you, my beloved. Take away your hand, I don't love you.

COMPLAINTE DE LA SEINE
(Lament of the Seine)

At the bottom of the Seine there is gold, and rusty boats, jewels, and weapons. In the depths of the Seine are the dead. There are tears, there are flowers nourished on slime and mud. There are hearts which suffered too well to live, and pebbles and grey creatures, the soul of the sewer exhaling poison from its mouth. There are rings tossed in by the misunderstood, and the feet of a cadaver sliced by a propeller. And the accursed fruits of a sterile womb, the unloved and aborted, the city's vomit. All this rests at the bottom of the Seine. Oh merciful Seine, the cadavers' home; oh bed with linen of slime, river of garbage with neither beacon nor harbor; singer who lulls the morgue and the bridges; welcome the poor, the woman, the drunkards, the demented. Mingle their sobs with the sound of your waves, and carry their hearts among the pebbles.

Nanna's Lied
(1939)

Words by
Bertolt Brecht

Music by
Kurt Weill

1. Mei-ne Her-ren, mit sieb-zehn Jah-ren kam ich
2. geht man mit den Jah-ren leich-ter

auf den Lie-bes-markt und ich ha-be viel er-
auf den Lie-bes-markt und um-armt sie dort in

fah-ren. Bö-ses gab es viel doch das war das Spiel. A-ber
Scha-ren. A-ber das Ge-fühl wird er staun-lich kühl wenn man

man-ches hab ich doch ver-argt. (Spoken) *(Schließlich bin ich ja auch ein Mensch.)*
da-mit all-zu-we-nig kargt. (Spoken) *(Schließlich geht ja jeder Vorrat zu Ende.)*

1,2 Gott sei

Dank geht al-les schnell vor-ü – ber auch die Lie-be und der Kum-mer so-

gar. Wo sind die Trä – nen von ge-stern a – bend? Wo ist der

Schnee vom ver-gan-ge-nen Jahr? Wo sind die Trä – nen von ge-stern

a – bend? Wo ist der Schnee vom ver-gan-ge-nen Jahr? 2. Frei-lich

3

ü – ber, auch die Lie - be und der Kum-mer so - gar._____ Wo sind die

Trä - nen von ge -stern a - bend? Wo ist der Schnee_____ vom ver-gan - ge -nen

Jahr? Wo sind die Trä - nen von ge -stern a - bend? Wo ist der

Schnee_____ vom ver-gan-ge -nen Jahr?_____

Complainte de la Seine
(1934)

Words by
Maurice Magre

Music by
Kurt Weill

larmes.... Au fond de la Sei - ne, il y a des fleurs; De vase et de boue, ell's sont nour-

ries... Au fond de la Sei - ne, il y a des cœurs Qui souf-frir'nt trop pour vi - vre la

vie... Et puis des cail - loux et des bê - tes gri - ses... L'â - me des é-

gouts souf-flant des poi - sons... Les an - neaux je - tés par des

in - com - pri - ses, Des pieds qu'une hé -li - ce a cou - pés du tronc...

Et les fruits mau-dits des ven - tres sté - ri - les, Les

blancs a - vor-tés que nul n'ai - ma... Les vo -mis - se-ments de la grand' vil - le... Au

fond de la Seine, il y a ce - la... O Sei - ne clé - men - te où vont les ca -

8

Klops Lied
(1925)

Traditional Berlin Folk Rhyme

Giocoso (♩ = 112)

Kurt Weill

Ick sit - ze da   un' es - se Klops

uff ee - mal klopp's   Ick kie - ke, stau - ne,

wun- dre mir, uff ee - mal jeht 'se uff, die Tür.

Na - nu, denk ick, ich denk: na - nu

jetzt is 'se uff, erscht war 'se zu!

Berlin im Licht-Song
(1928)

Words and Music by Kurt Weill

ist 'ne ziem-li-che Stadt. _____ Da - mit man da ___ al - les gut

se - hen kann, ____ da braucht man schon _ ei - ni - ge Watt. _____

_ Na _ wat denn? Na _ wat denn? Was _ is das für 'ne Stadt denn?

Refrain

Komm, mach mal Licht, da-mit man sehn kann, ob was da ist, komm, mach mal Licht und

re - de nun mal nicht. Komm, mach mal Licht, dann wol-len wir doch auch mal se - hen,

ob das 'ne Sa-che ist:_____ Ber - lin im Licht. Komm, mach mal Licht, da - mit man

sehn kann, ob was da ist, komm, mach mal Licht und re - de nun mal

nicht. Komm, mach mal Licht, dann wol - len wir doch auch mal se - hen,

ob das 'ne Sa - che ist:_____ Ber - lin im Licht.

Und was bekam des Soldaten Weib?

(1943?)

Words by
Bertolt Brecht

Music by
Kurt Weill

Moderato (♩ = 116)

1. Und was be-kam des Sol-da-ten Weib? aus der al-ten Haupt-stadt Prag? Aus
2. Und was be-kam des Sol-da-ten Weib? aus Brüs-sel im bel-gi-schen Land? Aus

Prag be-kam sie die Stö-ckel-schuh, ei-nen Gruß und da-zu die
Brüs-sel be-kam sie die sel-ten-en Spi-tzen, ach, das zu be-si-tzen, die

mf

Stö - ckel - schuh das be - kam sie aus der Stadt Prag.
bel - gi-schen Spi-tzen, die be - kam sie aus bel-gi-schem Land.

Und was be-

kam des Sol-da - ten Weib

1. aus___ Os - lo ü - ber dem Sund?
2. aus der Lich - ter - stadt Pa - ris?

Aus
Aus Pa -

p

Os - lo be-kam sie das Kräg - lein aus Pelz,___ hof-fent-lich ge - fällt's, das___
ris be - kam sie das sei - de - ne Kleid. Zu der Nach - ba-rin Neid das___

Kräg - lein aus Pelz, Das be - kam sie aus Os - lo am Sund.
sei - de - ne Kleid das be - kam sie___ aus___ Pa - ris.

Und was be-

kam des Sol - da - ten Weib

aus dem reich - en Am - ster -
aus dem süd - li - chen Bu - ka -

dam?
rest?

Aus Am - ster - dam be - kam sie den Hut und er
Aus Bu - ka - rest be - kam sie das Hemd so___

steht ihr gut, der hol - län - di - sche Hut den be - kam sie aus Am - ster -
bunt und so fremd, das ru - mä - ni - sche Hemd, das be - kam sie aus Bu - ka -

rit.

a tempo, ma più tranquillo *p*

dam.
rest.

Und was be -

f

rit.

p

kam des Sol - da - ten Weib aus dem wei - ten Rus - sen -

land? Aus_ Rus - sen-land be - kam sie den Wit - wen - schlei - er. Zu der

To - ten - fei - er den Wit - wen - schlei - er, das be - kam sie aus Rus - sen -

land, das be - kam sie aus Rus - sen - land.

rit.

Die Muschel von Margate

Petroleum-Song
(1928)

Words by
Felix Gasbarra

Music by
Kurt Weill

mal - te Mu - scheln an. Ganz Mar - gate kann - te sein Ge - bell:
ei - nen an - dern La - den an: ein Naph - ta und Ben - zin Kar - tell:
wur - de aus Blut Ben - zin; aus tau - send Häl - sen sprang der Quell:
tro - le - um heißt un - ser Va - ter - land, da - für zer - lö - chern wir uns das Fell:

Shell! Shell! Shell! Mu - schel von
Shell! Shell! Shell! Mu - schel von
Shell! Shell! Shell! Mu - schel von
Shell! Shell! Shell! Mu - schel von

Mar - gate bringt Ih - nen Glück, Mu - schel im gol - de - nen
Mar - gate brach - te ihm Glück, Mu - schel im gol - de - nen
Mar - gate bringt Ih - nen Glück, Mu - schel im gol - de - nen
Mar - gate bringt Ih - nen Glück, wir a - ber geh'n vor die

Wie lange noch?
(1944)

Words by
Walter Mehring

Music by
Kurt Weill

1. Ich will's dir ge-stehn, es war ei-ne
glaubt, ich war wie im

Nacht, da hab ich mich wil-lig dir hin-ge-
Wahn, von all dei-nen Re-den, von dei-nen

ge-ben, du hast mich ge-habt mich von Sin-nen ge-
Schwü-ren. Was im-mer du woll-test, das hab ich ge-

bracht, ich glaub-te, ich könn-te nicht oh-ne dich
tan. Wo-hin du auch woll-test, da ließ ich mich

le - ben. Du hast mir das Blau - e vom Him - mel ver - spro - chen und ich ha - be
füh - ren. Du hast mir das Blau - e vom Him - mel ver - spro - chen und ich! Ach ich

dich wie 'nen Va - ter ge - pflegt. Du hast mich ge - mar - tert, hast mich zer - bro - chen. Ich hätt dir die
hab' nicht zu wei - nen ge - wagt. Doch du hast dein Wort, dei - ne Schwü - re ge - bro - chen. Ich ha - be ge -

Er - de zu Füs - sen ge - legt. Sieh mich doch an! Sieh mich doch
schwie - gen und hab mich ge - plagt.

an! Wann kommt der Tag an dem ich dir sa - ge: es ist vor -

25

Youkali

Tango Habanera
(1935?)

Words by
Roger Fernay

M! de tango habanera

Music by
Kurt Weill

1. C'est presqu' au bout du mon -de, Ma bar-que va-ga-bon -de,
traî -ne, Las-san-te, quo-ti-dien -ne,

Er -rant au -gré de l'on -de, M'y con -dui -sit un jour.
Mais la pauvre âme hu-mai -ne, Cherch-ant par-tout l'ou -bli,

L'île est tou -te pe -ti -te,___ Mais la feé qui l'ha -bi -te
A, pour quit -ter la ter -re,___ Su trouv -er le mys -tè -re___

___ Gen -ti -ment nous in -vi -te___ A en fai -re le tour.___
___ Où nos rê -ves se ter -rent En quel -que You -ka -li.___

ka - li,____ C'est le pa - ys des beaux a - mours par - ta - gés,____ C'est l'es - pé - ran -

ce Qui est au cœur de tous les hu - mains,____ La dé - li - vran - ce Que nous at - tend - ons tous

pour de - main,____ You - ka - li,____ C'est_ le pa - ys de nos dé - sirs,

____ You - ka - li,____ C'est_ le bon - heur, c'est le plai - sir____ Mais c'est un rêve,

Der Abschiedsbrief
(1933?)

After the poem *Der Scheidebrief*
Erich Kästner

Music by
Kurt Weill

Zwei Stun-den sitz' ich schon im Ca - fé

Bau - er. Wenn Du nicht willst, dann sag mir's in's Ge - sicht. Des-we-gen wird mir mei - ne Milch nicht

©1977, 1981 by European American Music Corporation
International Copyright Secured
Text used by permission of the Estate of Erich Kästner

Printed in U.S.A.

sau - er, ich pfeif' auf Dich, mein Schatz, na schon, denn nicht. Du brauchst nicht

den-ken, daß ich Dich ent - beh - re, mit dem Ver - kehr mit mir, das ist jetzt aus! Auch ich hab'

so et - was wie ei - ne Eh - re. Laß Dich nicht blick - en, Schatz, laß Dich nicht

blick - en, Schatz, sonst fliegst Du 'raus! Du bist der

Er - ste nicht, der so ver - schwin - det. Das hab' ich nicht an Dir ver -

dient, mein gu - tes Kind! Du glaubst doch nicht daß sich nicht noch ein An - d'rer

fin - det? Es gibt noch wel - che, die be - que - mer für mich sind.

Ich hab' das Grü - ne an aus Pop-pe - lin. Das Loch d'rin hast Du auch hin - ein - ge -

ris - sen. Du weißt, es reicht mir nur bis zu den Knien. Ich hab' auch

noch ein an - ge - fan - g'nes Kis - sen. Das soll - test Du am Heil' - gen A - bend

krie - gen, das ist nun aus, und mir auch ei - ner - lei. Es wer - den

öf - ters An - dre da - rauf lie - gen, denn was vor - bei ist, Schatz, denn was vor -

bei ist, Schatz, das ist vor - bei! Du bist der

Er - ste nicht, der so ver - schwin - det. Das hab' ich nicht an Dir ver -

dient, mein gu - tes Kind. Du glaubst doch nicht, daß sich nicht noch ein An - d'rer

fin - det? Es gibt noch wel - che, die be - que - mer für mich sind.

schon. Der hat Mo - ne - ten, so ein al - ter Schie - ber. Be - halt dein

Geld, be - halt dein Geld, und schlaf al - lein, mein Sohn.

Auch Du bist ei - ner von die fei - nen Herrn.

Der Al - te kommt, er nimmt mich zu sich mit!

37

Es regnet
(1933)

Words by Kurt Weill
based on a suggestion by Jean Cocteau

Music by
Kurt Weill

©1977, 1981 by European American Music Corporation
International Copyright Secured

Buddy on the Nightshift

(from "Lunch Time Follies")
(1942)

Words by
Oscar Hammerstein II

Music by
Kurt Weill

Je ne t'aime pas
(1934)

Words by
Maurice Magre

Music by
Kurt Weill

soir, Trop in - ti - me - ment, à voix bas - se mêm'. Ne me don - ne pas sur - tout ton mou -
heur. Il me suf - fi - ra de voir ton sou - rir'. Con - te - moi com - ment il a pris ton

choir: Il ren - fer - me trop le par - fum que j'aim'. Dis - moi tes a - mours,
cœur Et mê - me dis - moi ce qu'on ne peut dir'... Non, tais - toi plu - tôt...

je ne t'ai - me pas,
Je suis à ge - noux...
Quelle heu - re te fut la plus en i -
Le feu s'est é - teint, la porte est fer -

vrant' Je ne t'ai - me pas...
mée... Je ne t'ai - me pas,
Et s'il t'ai - mait bien,
Ne de - man - de rien,

Spoken

Schickelgruber

(1942)

Words by
Howard Dietz

Music by
Kurt Weill

Allegro non troppo (𝅗𝅥 = 184)

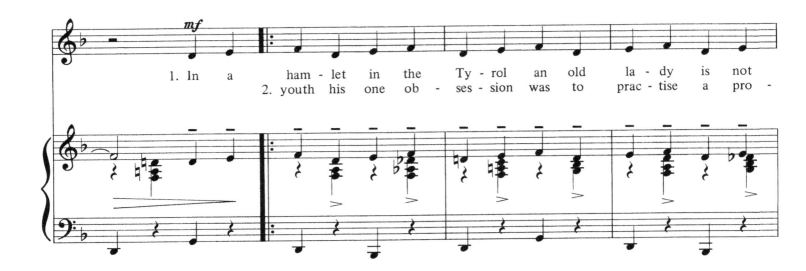

1. In a ham - let in the Ty - rol an old la - dy is not
2. youth his one ob - ses - sion was to prac - tise a pro -

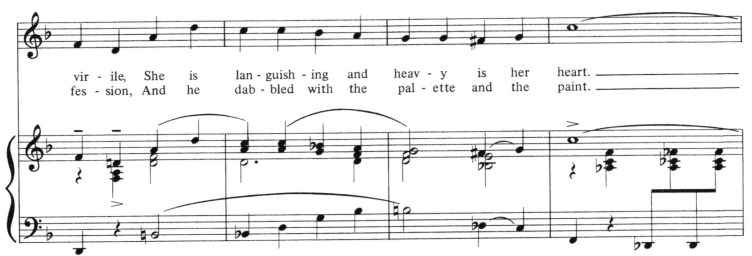

vir - ile, She is lan - guish - ing and heav - y is her heart.
fes - sion, And he dab - bled with the pal - ette and the paint.

For she thinks a - bout her
But the art he could - n't

ba - by who, had he been christ - ened A - bie, may - be might have nev - er
mas - ter, so he went from paint to plas - ter, and to - day he calls him -

played the mon - ster's part. _____ If her son had on - ly
self a plas - ter saint. _____ Is he good or e - vil

mar - ried, if her lust had not mis - car - ried, Who can say for cer - tain
fair - y? All his pals have now grown wa - ry, That is, those of them who

what might not have been.
did - n't rate the purge.

In her som - ber weeds of sor - row she is hope - ful some to-
And the scent will ev - er lin - ger, how he gave his friends the

mor - row will un - do the pas - sion that pro - duced a sin.
fin - ger just to grat - i - fy and cul - mi - nate an urge.

REFRAIN

Schick - el - gru - ber! Schick - el - gru - ber!
Schick - el - gru - ber! Schick - el - gru - ber!

54

love at thought of you!

2. In his vil - lage _____ that you pil - lage _____

_____ in re - venge will turn on you! _____

Das Lied von den braunen Inseln

Song of the Brown Islands
from Lion Feuchtwanger's "The Oil Islands"
(1928)

Words by
Lion Feuchtwanger

Music by
Kurt Weill

REFRAIN